CONTENTS

ACKNOWLEDGMENTS

To all the friends, family and colleagues who encouraged
me and gave of their time generously to comment and
advise in writing this book, especially my dear friend Ruth
for her professional guidance.
A special thanks to the congregation of Musselburgh
Congregational Church for being the first audience for
these reflections.

Foreword

Here is the familiar Christmas story, but in a context that will be fresh and new to many. Christmas is so deeply embedded in our culture that the richness of the story tends to be lost. Janice goes behind the feel-good story of the baby in the manger, behind the message of good will to all, behind the mystery of the angels and the wise men, to uncover the deeper mystery of God's purposes for the human race.

The whole of eternity is focused in the coming of Christ; God enters the cosmos He has made, bringing not just goodwill but forgiveness and salvation.

Janice sets this amazing context simply and clearly, and holds out to every person the promise of God's love. This would make a good resource for private reflection or group study, or as a way of reaching seekers.

Rev Dr Janet Wootton,
Witney, Oxfordshire
November 2017

JANICE ANDREWS

1 God's Plan for the Future Restoration of Shalom

In the book of Genesis, God creates life. Like a great craftsman, He weaves the threads of creation together, each one relating in millions of ways to the others until, like a beautiful tapestry, rich in diversity, in texture and in colour, the earth and everything upon it is created. (a)

God's dwelling place was among His people. The very first garden was a sanctuary where, in the presence of God, there was Shalom. The Hebrew world "Shalom" cannot be translated as simply "peace", its meaning runs so much deeper and richer than the word peace could ever describe. Shalom is complete wellbeing and harmony in every dimension of life, physical, emotional, social

and spiritual.   Shalom creates the climate in which
joy and peace may flourish.

This was God's plan for all creation, perfect
harmony. However, from the beginning, humanity
sought independence from God, to look beyond
God for other means of satisfaction, and, because of
this, the beautiful tapestry created by God was
damaged, threads were broken, Shalom was lost.

Self-centred aspirations of humanity led to greed,
materialism, poverty and crime, creating a climate
of uncertainty, suspicion and even fear.   In such a
climate it is not possible to have Shalom. Sadly, the
fall of mankind is not like a season of the year; it
does not pass, it is something that we live with
constantly. Harmony is broken, discord is here. The
tapestry of life is a mess.

God called His people Israel to be distinct, He gave
them laws in order for them to establish structured
and safe communities in the new land He was
giving them.   God's calling was for them to be
distinct and not to emulate the way of life of other
nations.   Therefore, they were not to marry into

pagan tribes, this would lead them astray. They were to look to God, and adhere to the laws and boundaries that He had given them. (b)

In due course, all of this went by the wayside. Once they were settled in the land, many Israelites were attracted to the lifestyles of those living in the nations around them, and they intermarried, in outright defiance of God's guidance. This led them into sexual misconduct, idolatry and even child sacrifice, which was widely practiced in the ancient world and which is abominable to God. (c)

The Israelites became far removed from how God had called them to live. The very fabric of their society was weak and vulnerable. Prophets repeatedly warned them to turn back to God, for failing to do so would lead them into the hands of their enemies. Sadly, warnings went unheeded, and these ominous prophesies came to pass. The land was invaded by the Babylonians and many were taken captive. The Israelites sat by the rivers of Babylon, and they wept for all they had lost. (d)

Israel's calling had been to be the people of God, to

seek justice, to encourage those who were oppressed, to defend the cause of the fatherless and plead the case of the widow, in other words, to seek Shalom for one another. (e)

Had Israel burned her bridges this time? Would there be any way back to God and to the land that He had promised? Even Solomon's magnificent Temple, which had been the beating heart of Jerusalem, had been razed to the ground. It was into this mood of despair and hopelessness that God raised up the Prophet Isaiah with a message of comfort and hope. God gave his word that He was preparing a new way forward. (f)

It wasn't too late for Israel, and it is never too late for us. God is gracious and forgiving. It is because of who He is that we always have hope. God describes this new road as His highway, the road that shall lead them home.

The Israelites were very familiar with the "King's Highway". This was the main trade route from Egypt, well-travelled by merchants of gold, precious oils, spices and fabrics. The route carved

its way through Egypt before crossing the Sinai
Desert, where the greatest danger to travellers was
intense heat by day and freezing cold by night.
Then the route wound its way through the ravines of
Petra in Jordan, where bandits hid in crevasses
waiting for the opportunity to attack traders and rob
them of their profits. So, although this promise
from God to create a new way forward is good news
and one of hope, the Israelites may also have felt
some trepidation. However, they have nothing to
fear, God promises to ease their passage. Hurdles
that rise up before them like mountains will be
brought low, valleys that are difficult to climb out
of will be raised up, and broken ground that could
cause them to stumble and fall will be levelled. (f)

Isaiah wonders how the Israelites would respond.
In the past they have struggled to be faithful; would
they continue to struggle in the future?   Their
fickle faith is compared to flowers that blossom but
only for a little while and then they droop, or like
grass that in time withers away. (g)

The good news for all of us is that God's promises
do not depend on our faithfulness, but on His. God
is faithful even when we are unfaithful. Knowing
this, Isaiah realizes Israel has nothing to fear, and he

cries out with joy "the word of God stands forever".
(h)

The beautiful imagery of Psalm 85 tells us that, in the fullness of time, Shalom will be realised. The Psalmist gives us a vision of perfection. Peace, justice, love and faithfulness will come together in wonderful intimacy, as if they are meeting in a kiss.
(i)

God was not prepared to leave His magnificent tapestry of creation in a tangled mess. He was not prepared to abandon us to the consequences of our sins. God's love for us is so great. It was the desire of His heart to redeem us, to reconcile us to Himself that we may know perfect peace, perfect love, and rest in the beauty of Shalom.

In the past God had spoken to the world through His laws, He had raised up Kings, and Judges, and then there followed a series of Prophets. However, this time He would not send a representative. The time had come for God to come in person, and He came in the person of His Son, Jesus Christ, the Light of the World. The rebellion of humanity had brought darkness and chaos, but light shines in the darkness and the darkness shall not overcome it. (j)

This is the joy and hope of Christmas

"For God so loved the world, that He gave His one
and only Son, that whoever believes in Him, shall
not perish, but have eternal life". (k)

Scripture Reference

a) Genesis 1 – 2: 1
b) 1 Kings 11: 1 – 3
c) Jeremiah 19: 5
d) Psalm 137: 1
e) Isaiah 1: 17
f) Isaiah 40: 3 – 5
g) Isaiah 40: 6 – 7
h) Isaiah 40: 8
i) Psalm 85
j) John 1: 1 – 5
k) John 3: 16

2 The Christ Child Foretold by the Prophets

The auditorium resounded to the swelling harmonies of the Scottish Symphony Orchestra. The emotions of the audience soared in unison as the rousing Beethoven symphony reached a magnificent crescendo.   When the orchestra came to the end of the piece, there was absolute silence. It was a momentary silence, but it was audible, and, in fact, it felt necessary and appropriate.   In the silence, the music continued to resonate.   It was as if the music was being given breathing space, giving listeners time to fully appreciate the beauty of what they had just heard, before the silence was broken by their thunderous applause.

This reminded me of the silence at the end of the Old Testament. The last book of the Old Testament leaves us on a cliff-hanger. Malachi prophesies the day that is coming, when God will send His Messiah into the world. It will be a time of great joy and salvation. He gives us such a beautiful illustration of young calves released into the fields for the first time. They have been cooped up throughout the long winter months but, at last, they are led out of their dark, confined stalls and can roam freely in rich green open pastures. The calves are so happy that they leap with joy. It is this abundant joy that Malachi foretells will be heralded in by the Messiah. (a)

The book of Malachi closes, and silence descends; a silence which is to last 400 years. However, it was not an empty silence. God's promises resonated with hope and expectation throughout these years as his faithful people waited in expectation for the Messiah to come into the world. The Prophet Isaiah describes this hope, not only as salvation for all God's faithful people, but a transformation so powerful that it can only be understood as a new creation.

Most of us have watched with fascination the amazing nature programmes produced by the esteemed Sir David Attenborough. Through the power of photography, we see the transformation that flourishes when the winter rains fall on the desert plains. What at first appeared to be a lifeless, barren wilderness is soon transformed to a sea of green, teeming with life.

We are shown a similar illustration by Isaiah when He describes the transforming power of the Messiah. The desert will blossom with flowers, there will be an abundance of greenery when springs of running water satisfy the thirsty land. The once deserted land will be a safe pathway for God's people, there are no dangers on the way, the blind will see, the deaf will hear and the lame will leap like deer. Those who are saved by God will sing songs of everlasting joy, as sorrow and mourning disappears, and they will be overcome by joy and gladness. (b)

What beautiful imagery of the wonderful hope that will be found in and through the King who is coming into the world. What kind of King would

He be? For years the Israelites had suffered at the hands of kings who were corrupt; they had plundered the poor and crushed the very people God had called them to serve.   This is God's condemnation of their leadership "I have found you grinding the faces of the poor". (c)

This new King will be like a fresh green shoot coming from the stump of Jesse. Jesse was the father of King David, the greatest king Israel had ever seen.   King David had brought unity to the nation; he had governed with justice and righteousness. He was the King whom God described as a man after His own heart. But not even David could compare to the King who was to come.   This King would be not only for Israel, but for the world.   He will not judge by what He sees or hears. He shall not be influenced by outward appearances.   He will judge the needy with righteousness and the poor with justice. (d)

He will know the very hearts of His people. (e) He will never be open to bribery. He cannot be bribed, for He desires or needs nothing for Himself. He will not be influenced by wealth or any earthly power or position.   Neither will He be swayed by the opinions of others.   He will be called Prince of

Peace. He will not be a King who expects others to serve Him; He will be a servant King, who will give His life for the world. (f)

This was the great hope instilled in the heart of Israel, generations before the birth of Christ. As a nation they pressed on, believing that God's word would come to pass. This is what hope does; hope presses on. In an underground tunnel, when all that can be seen is a glimmer of light in the far distance, those in the tunnel will step out in faith to move towards it. Faith and hope go together, hand and glove.

Not long after she lost her child, a mother posed for a great artist. In the painting, she is bent over, her body broken by sorrow and grief. Beside her is a large globe of the world, but she cannot see it for she has a blindfold across her eyes. This covering of her eyes is symbolic of the fact that her world has been lost and she cannot see any future. She is holding on to a small harp in her arms, but all the strings are broken except for one. The overall theme of the painting is brokenness and despair, and yet the artist entitled his work "Hope". (g) The one strand still intact on her harp signifies her faith in God. This is her hope and, as long as she has this strand of hope, she will have the strength to turn to

15

life and to the world once more.

Hope looks beyond time and sees eternity. Hope looks beyond present sufferings to future peace. Hope sees beyond temporary darkness to everlasting light. During this time of Advent, we wait once again to celebrate the coming of Christ into the world.   We look back to the promises of God and give thanks for the hope that resounded long and clear throughout the long periods of silence.   God's word goes out from His mouth and does not return to Him without accomplishing His purposes. (h)

May God bless you and your beloved this Christmas time.   His arms are outstretched towards you, offering you the most precious gift, the gift of His Son. He hopes that you will receive Him with gladness. Offer yourself as the cradle for the Christ child to be born within.   Open your heart that You may receive the richest blessings and know the deepest joy.

Scripture References
(a)   Malachi 4: 2
(b)   Isaiah 35: 5 – 10

(c)   Isaiah 3: 15
(d)   Isaiah 11: 1 - 10
(e)   John 2: 25
(f)   Mark 10: 45
(g)   "Hope" by George Frederic Watts,
(h)   Isaiah 55: 11

3 The 400-year Silence is Broken

Grief appears in many guises, many of which can only be understood when we have walked the road ourselves. When a young couple have longed for a child, only to be crushed by disappointment month after month, the suffering must seem unbearable. This had been the experience of Zechariah and Elizabeth. They had so longed for a child, and had prayed so sincerely asking God for this blessing. However, through time, they had come to accept that it was not to be.

Zechariah was now quite an old man, and Elizabeth was passed the age of child bearing. Added to the loss of their hope was the stigma that childlessness carried in the culture of the ancient Near East, making their sadness even harder to bear. However, through it all, they never doubted the wisdom and love of God. They served him lovingly and faithfully throughout their lives.

Zechariah was a priest in the rural community of Abijah in the hillsides of Judea. In a country less than half the size of Scotland, there were around 20,000 priests, split into different divisions. Each division took it in turn to travel to Jerusalem twice a year to carry out the duties of temple worship. This was considered a great honour.

It was the turn of Zechariah's division to set off on the journey to Jerusalem. Zechariah may have wondered which one of the men in his division would be chosen to enter into the sanctuary. Only one Priest was chosen to carry out these sacred duties. In order for everyone to have an equal opportunity to being chosen, their names were entered into a draw. Only those who'd never been chosen before were eligible to enter. This was, at best, a once in a lifetime experience.

Old Zechariah had been a Priest since the age of 30 and had never had this honour. We can only imagine his joy when it was his name was drawn! He had been selected to enter the sanctuary to burn incense outside the Holy of Holies, the most revered area of the temple, the place where God was believed to dwell.

The other Priests gather outside in prayer while Zechariah enters the temple and approaches the Holy place. He is alone. It is silent and it is very dimly lit. Suddenly, he is aware of a presence and he is gripped by fear when he sees an angelic figure standing by the altar. The Angel of God tells him not to be afraid; God has heard his faithful prayers. He and Elizabeth are to be blessed with a son who is to be called John. This child will be a great blessing; he will be filled with the Holy Spirit and he will draw people back to God. He is the one chosen by God to pave the way for the Lord. (a)

This is the voice that shatters 400 years of silence. A silence that had resonated with the promises of God. The last Old Testament prophet to speak was Malachi. It was through Malachi that God promised to renew His covenant, saying, "It will be a time of great joy and salvation, the sun of righteousness will rise with healing in its rays". (b) The time for this prophecy to be fulfilled was upon them, the Messiah was coming into the world.

God is often silent, but, in time, His promises always come to pass.

Let's ask ourselves "What is time"?

Time through the eyes of a child is perceived in a very different manner to how it is experienced by someone in later years. If you have ever travelled with a little one you will know that their constant cry is "are we there yet?" Time stretches out endlessly before them. It is very different for those in their twilight years for whom time passes so quickly. God's understanding of time is not like ours. For God, a day is like a thousand years, and a thousand years are like a watch of the night, but we can be sure that God's timing is always perfect. (c)

Zechariah lingers in the sanctuary. He is stunned as he wrestles with this prophecy. Can this possibly be true? He is an old man. Elizabeth is long past child-bearing age. The Angel of God seems perturbed at his word being questioned. It is as if he is saying, "Good grief, Zechariah! Do you not know that I am the Angel Gabriel? It is I who stand in the very presence of God. When I speak, I speak for God; to doubt me is to doubt God himself." With this rebuke, Zechariah was struck dumb and told that he would not speak until this prophecy was fulfilled. (d)

The Priests waiting outside were aware that something momentous had happened to Zechariah inside the Temple, but they were left to wonder what this could be for he could not tell them.

Within a month of Zechariah's return home, Elizabeth was with child. She spent most of her pregnancy in seclusion. However, we do know that she received one house guest; her young cousin, Mary. Mary came to tell her about her own miraculous pregnancy. When Mary enters her home, Elizabeth feels the child in her womb move as if he were leaping with joy.

Zechariah remained unable to speak until after his child was born. It was the day of the child's circumcision. Family, friends, and neighbours had all gathered together for this celebration. When it came to naming the child, everyone assumed that, in keeping with tradition, the baby would be called

Zechariah after his Father.   When Elizabeth said that the child was to be called John, they were all puzzled. No-one else in the family was called John. In sign language, the men ask Zechariah what he thinks; what would he like the child to be called? Zechariah asked for a writing tablet and wrote down that the child was to be called John. At that moment, God's prophecy was fulfilled, and Zechariah immediately regained his voice and began singing praises to God. (e)

Zechariah is overcome with joy. God is raising up a horn of salvation from the lineage of King David and it is his child, John, who has the mighty task to go before Him to prepare the way. John will teach people the message of salvation through the forgiveness of their sins. He will tell the world about the One who will guide our feet in the pathway of peace. (f)

God could have chosen any one of an array of different ways to herald Christ into the world.   He could have given voice to the wind, or rendered open the heavens, but He chose to act through the person of John the Baptist. This is how God accomplishes His purposes. He calls ordinary men and women to bear witness to the light of the

Gospel and to go forward in the world, bearing the torch of truth.

News of what had happened to Zechariah in the temple and the circumstances leading to the birth of his son spread through the hillside villages of Judea. Everyone was convinced that the hand of God was upon this child, John. They were interested to see what he would become, and they expected great things of him. For many years John the Baptist lived in the wilderness until it was time to herald the arrival of the Messiah.

There is a time for everything; God's timing is perfect. When the set time had come, God sent His Son into the world. (g)

When our hopes and dreams are lost and the vision that we had for our future is shattered, we stumble and grope, trying to make sense of it all. It is at times like these we long for God to speak, to reassure us, but God is calling upon us to trust Him in the silence. He is with us, and He is bringing His purposes to pass.

The Christ child is coming into the world

He shall be called Immanuel, "God with us" (h)

Scripture References

(a)   Luke 1: 5 - 17
(b)   Malachi 4: 2
(c)   Psalm 90: 4
(d)   Luke 1: 18 – 20
(e)   Luke 1: 57 – 64
(f)   Luke 1: 69 – 79
(g)   Galatians 4: 4
(h)   Matthew 1: 23

4 Beauty from Brokenness

There is great interest these days in the subject of genealogy. The TV programme "Who Do You Think You Are?" attests to the fact that, if we dig far enough back, we are likely to unearth surprises in our family tree Gary Lineker discovered that his great, great grandfather spent time in jail for stealing chickens. He had been so poor, he'd stolen six chickens to feed his family. Jeremy Paxman was reduced to tears when he heard of how his great, great grandmother had been denied the widow's pension on a technicality. She was left to bring up 9 children on her own in the slums of Glasgow. (a)

Jesus has some interesting characters in His own family tree. Jesus was raised in an ordinary family; a family with problems, regrets, challenges and difficulties. His ancestor, Rahab, had been a prostitute. She also had a heart of gold. God sent His men to find refuge in her home when they were at their most vulnerable. She took them in, and she gave them shelter, warmth and hospitality. She did this at considerable risk to herself. (b) God sees the heart, and what He saw in the heart of Rahab was abundant love and compassion for others.

Rahab had a son called Boaz. The story that unfolds is of how God brought a young woman called Ruth into the life of Boaz and into the family tree of our Lord.

The story of Ruth is only around four pages long, and yet it is packed full of life experiences and moves across the spectrum of emotion, from one extreme to another. The story follows a family who move from comfortable settlement to enforced change, from hope to despair, and from happiness to deep sadness. At their darkest moment, it is impossible to envisage life ever being good again. However this is the moment when light breaks through, allowing a glimpse of future joy. In good times and in bad, God is working out His purposes.

Family life is rarely like a clear, straight drive on the highway. More often than not, the road before us is full of twists and turns, with unexpected potholes and diversions along the way. Some situations stop us in our tracks completely, as if a landslide has blocked the road ahead, leaving us unsure of how we will make it through. When we cannot see a way ahead, it is often during these times that God is laying foundation stones for our future.

The book of Ruth opens with a family on the brink of a major decision. They live in Bethlehem, but a famine has come upon the land. Should they risk remaining where they are, or should they move to the neighbouring town of Moab? A leading politician, during a period of particularly high unemployment in Britain, used the slogan "get on your bike" to encourage people to go looking for work. However, for people who have only ever lived in one place throughout their lives, this is easier said than done. Belonging to a close-knit community is a source of comfort and security. Naomi and her husband, Elimelech, have two sons to consider, and their decision is to move. Gathering whatever possessions they can carry, the four of them set off to live in Moab until the famine is over.

At first their new life goes so well. The boys marry girls from the Moab community. Sadly, however, Elimelech dies, and Naomi is supported by her sons and daughters-in-law. However, there is a much greater blow to come. After 10 years of living in Moab, both of Naomi's sons die. She is devastated. She no longer wants to be known as Naomi; which in Hebrew means "pleasantness", instead she asks to be known as Mara, which means 'bitter'. Life had become so bitter and hard to bear; her tears were endless. (c)

Naomi feels there is no longer anything to keep her in Moab. She decides to return to Bethlehem. When she sets off, both daughters-in-law, Ruth and Orpah, start out on the journey with her, until they reach a point where she turns to them and tells them to go home. She can offer them nothing; in Bethlehem she has no male relatives to provide for them. Her life is over, but it's different for them; they are young, they can start again. She encourages them to go back to their own mothers, to their own community where they will be more likely to meet new husbands and start families of their own.

Both girls cling to Naomi, not wanting to leave her, but, eventually, Orpah kisses her goodbye and turns in the direction of Moab. However, Ruth refuses to abandon her mother-in-law. Naomi painted a very bleak picture of the future, and yet young Ruth was prepared to enter into this bleakness with her. She said, "Naomi, wherever you go, I will go, your people will be my people, your God will be my God. Wherever you die, that's where I too will die". So, together, they walk home to Bethlehem, (d) Naomi seeking what is best for Ruth, and Ruth seeking what is best for Naomi. Their love for one another fulfils Christ's commandment to love one another. (e)

When they eventually arrive in Bethlehem, there is pity in the expressions of those who remember Naomi from years earlier. She had left with a husband and two sons, and she now cut a very lonely figure returning without them. In a patriarchal society where women relied on men for everything, how on earth would these two women survive?

Ruth has to find a way of providing for them both. She offers to go to work in the fields. God's law provided for the poor, which meant that farmers did not harvest the edges of their fields. A border of grain was left for the poor to glean; it was here that

Ruth went to gather food. (f)

This is the point in the story when we see the providence of God breaking through. It transpires that the owner of the field, Boaz (g), is a distant relative of Naomi's dead husband, and, as it was the custom for widows to remarry within the family, we see a glimmer of hope that perhaps there may be a new husband for young Ruth after all. (h)

Boaz is a man of God. He tells his workers to leave Ruth alone, and to leave plenty of grain for her to glean. Ruth is quite overcome; life has been so hard, and now she is receiving such kindness. She asks Boaz, "Why is it that I have found favour in your eyes". He replies that it is because she is a woman of God. He has heard about everything she has done for Naomi; it speaks volumes about her character and her values. (h)

Ruth had left everything, expecting nothing other than to support Naomi, but God had many blessings for her future. Not only were Boaz and Ruth married, they were blessed with a son. Naomi, too, was blessed. She had lost the men in her life, but now she had a grandson. She was so happy. The villagers had all shared in her sadness, but now they shared in her great joy. (i)

This story does not stand in isolation; it is part of a much bigger plan that God was bringing to pass. The son of Ruth and Boaz was named Obed. He became the father of Jesse, Jesse was the father of King David (j), and Christ our everlasting King was born from David's line.

Through bereavement, uncertainty, desperation, and hopelessness, God was working out His purposes. The story of Ruth is testament to the fact that the greatest joys often come after we have ploughed through some very rough ground.

God calls us to make Him our vantage point.   He sees beyond the landslides.   He is creating new pathways for our future.

Ruth and Naomi experienced hardships and blessings. Throughout those good times and bad times, they were true to the two greatest commandments. They loved and trusted God, and they loved one another. They never made decisions based on what was best for the self, but always on what was best for the other. When love is reciprocal we see its perfection.

May God's perfect love embrace you and your family this Christmas time, and may He help you to trust that He is making all things new.

God is creating a new way, He makes streams in the desert and creates new pathways in the wilderness. (k)

Scripture References

(a)   www.bbc.co.uk/whodoyouthinkyouare/past-stories
(b)   Joshua 2: 1 – 15
(c)   Ruth 1: 3 – 5
(d)   Ruth 1: 16 – 17
(e)   John 13: 34 – 35
(f)   Leviticus 23: 22
(g)   Boaz was the beloved Son of Rahab
(h)   Ruth 2: 4 – 12
(i)   Ruth 4: 13 – 17
(j)   Matthew 1: 5 – 6
(k)   Isaiah 43: 19

5 *The Inauguration of the Kingdom of God on Earth*

The birth of Christ is the greatest event in the history of the world. In fact, the moment of His birth defines history. If you take an ice pick and tap the ice at this point, fissures shoot out in all directions like the points of a star, and the ice breaks at the centre of the star. At the moment of the birth of Christ, history breaks into two different eras at the centre of the star. The world of AD is one world and the world of BC is another.

In sending His Son into the world, God was communicating with humanity in a way that He had never done before. Throughout the years of the Old Testament, God raised up Prophets, all of whom were good men, obedient and faithful. They were privileged to speak the words that God had given them, and they acted as God's mouthpiece. However, no single one of them had full knowledge of God; their knowledge was always only part of the whole.

It was through Abraham that God's plan was revealed to establish a new nation of people. This would be the nation of Israel, from which the Messiah would come. (a) It was through Jacob that we learned that He would come from the tribe of Judah. (b) It was through Isaiah that we were told that the Messiah would come from the line of King David. (c) It was the prophet Micah who introduced us to John the Baptist, the forerunner, whose voice would call out in the wilderness. (d)

This partial knowledge of the prophets reminds us of the words of Paul from 1 Corinthians 13: 1 – 13 : "Where there is knowledge it will pass away, for we know in part and we prophesy in part but, when completeness comes, what is in part disappears". Christ is completeness, He is perfection. All the Prophets knew something of God, but only Jesus knows Him completely. Everything that had gone before, which at the time seemed wonderful, was now just a pale reflection. For in Jesus, God had made Himself fully known.

Jesus is the visible image of the invisible God.
When we look at the sun on a clear day we cannot
look at it without seeing its brightness.   Nor can we
look at Christ and not see the radiance of God, nor
look at God and not see the beauty of Christ for
they are One.   Through Christ all life is made. He
pre-exists the universe, He stands outside of space
and time.   There has never been a time when Christ
was not.   He is from eternity to eternity. (e)

For Jesus to come to earth and live among us, He
became fully human. This meant laying aside His
glory.   It was as if a veil was drawn over His
divinity, a veil of human flesh.   When we sing the
Christmas carol, 'Hark the Herald Angels Sing', we
say these very words, "veiled in flesh the Godhead
see, hail the incarnate Deity. Pleased as man with
man to dwell, Jesus our Immanuel".   In Christ, God
is with us. God came to earth in the humblest of
ways, as a new born babe.   He came to His own,
but His own did not receive Him. (f) Why was this?
Why did so many of His own not recognise Him?

Jesus was not the kind of Messiah that the Israelites
were expecting. He was known to come from

Nazareth, such a backwater, an insignificant place. Few knew that He was born in Bethlehem from where the Messiah was prophesised to come. (g) His parents were of lowly social standing, people of no significance. His father was a carpenter, and there had been talk of scandal at the time of Jesus' birth, rumours of illegitimacy!

The Israelites looked back to the glory days of King David. He was the greatest King that Israel had ever seen. Under his reign Israel had been unified and victorious. He was a warrior, a great military conqueror; how much greater would the Messiah be? At the time of the birth of Christ, Israel was under the dominion of the Roman Empire. The people longed to be free, to be independent from Rome, and they envisaged a Messiah who would accomplish this. They were awaiting a Messiah who would lead them in battle, a strong political figure, a force to be reckoned with, a King under whom Israel would once again be a great nation, free from Roman occupation.

Jesus did not fit this description. He was not the kind of King they were expecting. He was not political. He was not a warrior. He had no army, no weapons, no wealth, no possessions. What kind of Messiah was this?

Jesus is the King who rules with His heart. The nature of His Kingdom is love. He cares for the poor and the needy; under Him they shall have perfect justice. He is the source of peace for all mankind. His Kingdom is not bound by geographical boundaries, nor is it for a season. He shall reign over all nations and His rule shall be everlasting. This is our King.

Let us gather around the cradle of King Jesus this Christmas. God calls us to come just as we are. He asks nothing of us except that we come with open arms to receive His beautiful gift, and to go out into the world to tell others about the love, the hope, the joy and the peace that are found in our everlasting King.

Scripture References
(a)   Genesis 12: 2
(b)   Genesis 49: 8 – 10
(c)   Isaiah 9: 7
(d)   Micah 3: 1
(e)   Colossians 1: 15 – 20
(f).   John 1: 11
(g)   Micah 5: 2

6 The Faith and Trust of Mary and Joseph

Mary and Joseph were young and in love. Their betrothal to one another was arranged and agreed by their parents, as was the cultural norm of the time. The next step was to publicly announce their union, making it legally binding, able to be broken only by death or divorce. No intimacy was permitted during this time. Mary and Joseph respected and upheld this sexual purity law of God and Mary remained a virgin. All was well. The forthcoming marriage of this young couple was a source of joy to them both, and also to their families and the close-knit community of Nazareth.

A measure of our faith is in how we respond to

God.   How willing are we to step out in obedience?
How do we react when God's call is very
demanding? What happens when those demands
not only impact our own lives but also have difficult
consequences for those we love?   How sensitive
are we to the opinions of others, when God's call
raises eyebrows in our community and exposes us
to scrutiny and criticism? I wonder if some of these
doubts and fears raced through Mary's mind when
she was called by God to bear His son!

The Angel Gabriel came to Mary and told her that
she was highly favoured, but Mary didn't feel
favoured at all; she was "greatly troubled" (a)   How
could this be? How will she tell Joseph? What will
he think of her? What about her Mum and Dad, and
perhaps even worse, what about his Mum and
Dad!!! What on earth would people think?   What
about all their plans for the wedding!!!

Even when we love and trust God, often our very
human response to the many challenges and
changes we face in life, is to hesitate, to focus on
the negatives, the 'what if's, running through all the
obstacles which now confront us.   However, as our
faith matures, and as we experience again and
again, God's perfect wisdom, His perfect

faithfulness and His abundant love, we learn to trust
Him completely even when we cannot see the way
ahead, nor understand His plans.   God's thoughts
are not our thoughts, neither are our ways, His
ways. (b)

Being yoked to God does not guarantee an easy
path, but it does assure a path of goodness, wisdom
and truth. God can be trusted in every situation, He
hopes that we will follow with the trust of a little
child.   A 5 year old who spent every Saturday
helping his Grandad on the farm was distraught one
day when his Mum said he couldn't go. He said to
his Mum, "But I have to go, Grandad says he
doesn't know what he would do without me"!!!
God doesn't need us, He loves us, and He delights
when we desire to play our part in the work of His
Kingdom.

The Angel Gabriel is aware of Mary's very human
vulnerability and seeks to reassure her by bringing
her cousin Elizabeth into the conversation.   God
was working out His purposes in her life too!
Elizabeth had been well past child bearing age when
God promised her husband Zechariah that they
would be blessed with a Son, and now Elizabeth
was in her sixth month of pregnancy; proof, if proof

were needed, that God's word prevails, and that
what God ordains shall always come to pass. (c)

Mary's fears turn to astonished joy as she realises
the wondrous miracle that is happening in her life.
Of all the young girls throughout the whole of
Judea, God has chosen her to bear His Son!   How
can this be, she is so lowly so ordinary? She is poor,
in the eyes of the world. She is insignificant, but not
in the eyes of God. God sees the heart (d) and what
He sees in Mary is a heart full of faith.

So too was the heart of Joseph. What must Joseph
have thought when he heard of Mary's pregnancy?
He knows the child is not his, for there has been no
intimacy between them.   He must have been
confused and troubled, but he shows no anger or
resentment. His immediate concern was for Mary
only. News of her pregnancy will cause a scandal in
their small community, exposing Mary to public
shame and disgrace. This is what concerns Joseph.
He wants to protect her as much as he possibly can
and decides that the best course of action for him to
take is to seek a divorce as quietly as possible. (e)

However, that night in his sleep, Joseph is reassured by an Angel of God who comes to him, telling him that Mary is speaking the truth. Her conception is of God, the work of His Holy Spirit. Joseph must not be filled with doubts or fears, but be full of faith, he should take Mary to be his wife. When the child is born, He is to be called Jesus. Jesus is Hebrew for "Joshua" which means "God Saves"; this little one is the Saviour of the world. (f)

The story draws out like a beautiful symphony, gradually rising to this beautiful crescendo of love and faith that possess this young couple.

The first-person Mary tells is her cousin Elizabeth. Not only do they share being pregnant, but Elizabeth is also woven into God's plan for the salvation of the world. She is carrying John the Baptist, the little child who will be born to pave the way for the Messiah. When the two women greet one another, Elizabeth feels her baby move, it is as if he is leaping for joy in her womb. Elizabeth refers to Mary as the Mother of her Lord and Mary bursts into a song of thankfulness. (f) What a wonderful story of love, of trust and of faith, and what wonderful hope for the world. The Saviour of the world is coming.

God's hand is outstretched towards us this Christmas time. It is the desire of His heart to bring His purposes to pass through ordinary people, like you and like me. He hopes that we will have ears to hear His call, and hearts of faith, willing to respond as Mary and Joseph did in perfect obedience.

Put your hand in the hand of the Master and stride out with confidence, not knowing what the future holds, but trusting in the One Who holds the future.

Scripture References
(a)   Luke 1: 28 – 30
(b)   Isaiah 55: 8
(c)   Luke 1: 36 – 37
(d)   1 Samuel 16: 7
(e)   Matthew 1: 18 – 19
(f)   Luke 1: 39 – 56

7 Christ is born in Bethlehem

Mary was in the advanced stages of pregnancy.
Very soon her baby would be born. Ideally this
would have been a time to rest in preparation for the
birth.   However, the decision of Caesar Augustus to
call a census of every household put paid to any
notion of resting!   It was the custom for a census to
be taken every 14 years. This ensured that there was
a register of all men eligible for military service,
and also provided a register of all those liable to pay
taxes to Rome. (a)

Caesar Augustus was completely oblivious to the
fact that God was weaving his secular plans to
enrich and strengthen the Roman Empire into God's
own plan for the Salvation of the world.

The order was given for all men who were no longer residing in the land of their tribes to return there to register for the census. This is why Joseph and Mary had to go to Bethlehem, the town of Joseph's ancestors, the town of King David from whose line the Christ child would come. The place of Christ's birth was prophesied 700 years earlier: "Bethlehem, though you are small among the clans of Judah, out of you will come one who will be ruler over Israel, whose origins are from of old, from ancient times." (b)

The distance from Nazareth to Bethlehem was 80 miles. It would be a difficult and worrying journey for the young couple to make. How panicked must they have felt when they eventually arrived in Bethlehem with Mary now in labour? They were desperate for shelter. Under normal circumstances this would not have been a problem in Bethlehem, but, because so many had travelled there to participate in the census, the population had swelled greatly and all rooms were taken.

An innkeeper offered them the use of the stable, the rough shelter for his animals. This is where Mary gave birth to the child. She wrapped Him in strips of cloth, and laid Him in a manger, which was an animal feeding trough. (c)

It is very moving and challenging to be told that Mary and Joseph could find no room for Christ to be born. It is a rebuke upon humanity. Throughout Christ's life, people failed to make room for Him. When His disciples asked what it would mean to follow Him, Jesus replied "Foxes have dens, birds have nests, but the Son of Man has nowhere to lay His head". (d)

The world today is crying out for love, for peace, for truth, all of which is found in Christ, and yet still there are many who have no room for Him. Christ longs for us to offer our lives to Him that He may enter in and be born in us this day.

As Christ was laid in the manger, out on the nearby hills some shepherds were tending their flocks. It is hugely significant that the first people to hear the good news of the birth of Christ were shepherds. Jesus is the Good Shepherd who will lay down His life for His flock. (e) However, there is an even greater, but much more ominous, significance.

In the Temple of Jerusalem, both morning and evening, unblemished lambs were offered for sacrifice. These sacrificial lambs came from flocks raised on the hillsides of Bethlehem. It is very likely, therefore, that the shepherds were tending the very lambs that, in time, would be taken to Jerusalem to be sacrificed. Christ was born to die. The visit from the Shepherds points to the cross, where Christ offers Himself as the pure unblemished lamb of God, sacrificed for the sins of the world.

When the shepherds first receive the good news of the Messiah's birth, they are terrified. They were out in the darkness and stillness of the open countryside at night, when suddenly the light of God shone around them and an angel appeared, telling them not to be afraid, for it is good news: the Messiah has been born! The shepherds will find Him in the town of David, in Bethlehem. He will be wrapped in cloths and lying in a manger. He has come to bring joy to all humanity. A whole host of angels cry "Glory to God in the highest, and on earth peace to those on whom His favour rests". (f)

The story of the birth of Jesus is as lowly as it gets. An 80-mile trek over dusty open countryside, only to find no proper shelter for a woman who is already in labour! The poorest and grubbiest of birthing surroundings, with only a feeding trough to lay the child, and lowly shepherds to visit Him! Jesus is King, but He is not a king raised in privileged surroundings. He was exposed to the dirt and grime of life, but the dirt and grime never tarnished nor diminished Him in any way. He has come to transform the dirt and grime of the world into something beautiful and everlasting.

In accordance with Jewish customs, Jesus was circumcised at 8 days old. After the 40-day purification period, which women observed after giving birth, Mary and Joseph took Him to the temple to dedicate him to God. The consecration of a child was made with an offering of a lamb. However, in circumstances of poverty, parents could offer a pair of doves or pigeons; and this was Mary and Joseph's offering, reflecting their lowly social status - and yet they were rich beyond measure!

At the temple, there was a man called Simeon. He had been promised by God, that he would not die before he had seen the Messiah. That moment had come. God kept His promise. Simeon took the Christ child in his arms and said "Sovereign God,

You can now dismiss Your servant in peace, for my eyes have seen Your salvation". (g)

The joy of Simeon is our joy this Christmas time. Christ is God's gift to the world, a gift to treasure, but we must choose to receive Him.

May you respond by asking the Christ child to be born in you tonight that His dwelling place may be at the very core of your being. Then you shall go out with joy, and be filled with peace.

Fix your eyes upon Jesus, and give thanks to God with the words of Simeon "my eyes have seen Your salvation" (g).

Thanks be to God for His gift to the world.

Scripture References
a) Luke 2: 1 – 5
b) Micah 5: 2
c) Luke 2: 7
d) Luke 9: 57 – 58
e) John 10: 11

f)   Luke 2: 8 – 9
g)   Luke 2:30

8 *Faith sees beyond the horizons of our sight*

The Civil Rights activist Martin Luther King had a wonderful vision of how life would be - not how life *could* be, but *would* be. Even though the immediate circumstances of his people remained very difficult, he didn't allow the everyday reality of his current situation - the oppression and denial of basic civil rights - to limit his hopes or his dreams for the future.   He saw beyond the horizons of his sight, believing, that what he hoped for, longed for, believed in, would surely come to pass. This is the exact description that is given to faith in the book of Hebrews chapter 11. It reads: "Faith is being confident in what we hope for and being assured of what we do not yet see."[a]

To have this certainty of faith in our lives is

powerful. It sustains us and upholds us. Even in the midst of our greatest difficulties, faith sees, hopes and believes in light when all around us there is darkness.

As the great spokesman of the civil rights movement, Martin Luther King shared his vision of racial equality in his speech: "I have a dream" which he delivered in August 1963. In it he quotes directly from Isaiah chapter 40: (b) "I have a dream that one day every valley shall be exalted, and every hill and mountain shall be made low, the rough places will be made plain, and the crooked places will be made straight; and the glory of the Lord shall be revealed and all flesh shall see it together." This word of God spoken through Isaiah reveals the hope that is coming into the world through the Messiah and the justice and righteousness that His reign will herald in the world.

Martin Luther King believed that racism, injustice, oppression and abuse of power would be defeated. They would not prevail when confronted by those seeking the Kingdom of God. Jesus is the King of righteousness, He seeks justice for all humanity, irrespective of race, religion culture or colour.

In the 5 years that followed, Martin Luther King's dream was not fulfilled. In fact nothing much changed; racism, oppression and abuses continued, but Martin Luther King kept the faith. On the 3rd of April 1968, he gave another wonderful speech based on the story of Moses. Moses is the great leader of Israel, raised up by God to lead the Israelites to the promised land, but he himself does not enter it. God leads him to the top of Mount Nebo where Moses sees the whole land before him, but he never steps foot on its soil. (c)

Martin Luther King would never know how prophetic the words of his great speech would be that night. He said this, "God has allowed me to go up to the mountain, and I've looked over, and I've seen the Promised Land. I may not get there with you, but I want you to know tonight, that we, as a people, will get to the promised land! I am so happy tonight, I'm not fearing any man. Mine eyes have seen the glory of the coming of the Lord". The next day, Martin Luther King Jr. was shot in the neck by an assassin's bullet.

God uses people of great faith to bring His purposes

to pass.

Mary's calling to bear the Messiah exposed her to the risk of rejection, public ridicule and disgrace and yet she responded to God with these words "I am your servant Lord, whatever You say, I will do." [d]

The easy route for Joseph would have been to divorce Mary and move on with his life, but Joseph is also convinced that this conception is of God and he ,too, is obedient. No doubt they were both aware of wagging tongues, but the voice they heard and obeyed was the voice of God.

When the child was born it must have been wonderful for them to have their faith confirmed by the men who had come down from the hills, for they too had been told that this little one was the Messiah, and they believed. Mary and Joseph had been right to trust, and they would continue to trust. The word was beginning to spread out into the wider world, the message that this child was the Son of God.

It is at the temple in Jerusalem, that Mary and

Joseph encounter Simeon and Anna. Anna had been widowed after only 7 years of marriage. She was now 84 years old, and her life had been dedicated to serving in the temple. Simeon was an old man, but years earlier he had been promised by God that the Messiah would come in his lifetime. Simeon never failed to believe that this would come to pass.

If we were to stand on the side of a mountain, we would only see what is visible immediately around us. For us to be able to see what lies on either side of the mountain would require us to make our way to the ridge of the summit; only on the mountain top would we see the whole view.

Simeon and Anna were privileged to stand on the mountain ridge of history. They could look back on the hope shared with generations of Israelites. Now, with the arrival of this little child, they could look to the future with joy, convinced that this child was the Messiah, believing that through Him all of God's promises would come to pass.

Simeon warned Mary, that the joy she was experiencing now would be equaled or surpassed by her agony in years to come. Just as Mary had been prepared to carry and give birth to this child, she was already being prepared for the realisation that she would need to share Him with the world and ultimately, she would suffer the agony of His loss. (e)

This Christmas, we stand with Anna and Simeon on the ridge of the mountain summit with a view of the big picture. The ancient prophecies of God are fulfilled in the coming of the Saviour of the world. Let us acclaim with joy: "Mine eyes have seen the glory of the coming of the Lord."

May God bless you and keep you this Christmas time.

May He lift up His face to shine upon you.

May He be gracious unto you.

May God lift up His countenance upon you,

And give you peace

Scripture References

a)   Hebrews 11: 1
b)   Isaiah 40: 4 – 5
c)   Deuteronomy 34: 4
d)   Luke 1: 38
e)   Luke 2: 34

9 The Magi

In the ancient world there were no street lamps to light the way; people navigated their journeys by looking to the stars.   There was a general belief that a person's destiny was linked to the star under which they were born.   Astrologers studied the constellations believing that, when any unusual phenomenon in the heavens was discovered, this indicated that something equally extraordinary must be happening on Earth.   The Magi were part of the ancient eastern world of astronomy which blended with astrological thinking.

For centuries, scientists have tried to figure out which factors contributed to the formation of the exceptional star, whose brightness convinced the Magi of a unique happening in the world.   At that time in history the planets of Saturn and Jupiter were in conjunction with one another and this may have given the appearance to those on earth of a super star. Saturn was believed to have had special relevance for the Jews, and Jupiter represented royalty, in fact it was known as the Royal planet. The correlation of these two planets and their combined symbolism may have signified to the Magi that a new Jewish King had been born.

The Magi followed the star until they came to Jerusalem. Jerusalem is the Jewel in Israel's crown. It is the seat of political power and the focus of religious authority. To the Magi, it would have seemed like the most obvious place to look for the new King. This was where King Herod had his palace. Not in their wildest dreams would the Magi expect a King to be born in the poorest of poor circumstances in the backwater town of Bethlehem, surrounded only by humble, rural dwellings.

In Jerusalem the Magi began asking of people, "Where is the one who has been born king of the Jews? We saw his star when it rose and we have come to worship him." (a)

Politically, this statement was dynamite! Herod the Great was the reigning King of the Jews. He had been given the title by the Roman Senate, some 40 years previously. Since that time, he had become increasingly paranoid about even a hint of any threat to his rule, so much so that three of his own sons were put to death for treason. (b)

When word reaches Herod of the Magi who have travelled from an Eastern Nation and who are asking many curious questions about a newly born King of the Jews, he is deeply concerned. He sends for the priests and teachers of the law, and asks them where the Messiah was expected to be born. This reveals his ignorance! He is not familiar with the ancient Jewish scriptures. Herod himself was not fully Jewish, and was not popular with the Jewish people. He curried favour with them through his magnificent building projects, particularly his rebuilding of the magnificent temple in Jerusalem, but generally he was feared and despised.

The priests and teachers of the law answer Herod's question, replying "Bethlehem". (c)

Dark and ominous scheming emerge in what Herod does next. He sends for the Magi. He conceals his true feelings, and engages in conversation with them about the new King. He asks them specifically about when the star had first appeared. This was so that he could determine the exact age of the child. He advises them to go to Bethlehem. However, he asks that, whenever they find this King, they must return to Jerusalem and share the news with him. He wants to know exactly where to find him, so that he too may go to him and pay homage. (d)

The Magi set off and follow the star until they reach Bethlehem. At last they come to the cradle of the Christ child. The precious gifts they have brought with them are all symbolic of who Christ is.

Frankincense was the incense used by the priests in temple worship: this gift points to the Priesthood of Christ. He is the High Priest (e) who intercedes for us before the very throne of God. (f)

Gold speaks of the Kingship of Jesus.

Myrrh was a spice or balm used in preparing bodies for burial. This gift points to His atoning death.

When the time came for the Magi to leave Bethlehem and make the long journey homeward, they were warned in a dream not to return via Jerusalem. They were to ignore King Herod's command to return and inform him of the location of the Messiah. Instead, they were instructed to return to their country by another route. (g)

Mary, Joseph, and the Christ child were now in grave danger. King Herod would stop at nothing to find the child and have Him put to death, since only murder of the child could guarantee the elimination of any threat to his rule! Joseph also had a dream in which he was warned to take Mary and the Christ child and flee to Egypt. This fulfils another prophecy "out of Egypt I called my Son" (h)

Herod was enraged when he realised that he had been duped by the Magi. He commanded all infant boys, under the age of two, in Bethlehem to be put to death, thus safely eradicating any potential pretender to his throne. (i) Questions have been asked as to why this slaughter is not recorded in the history books of its time. One possible explanation has been suggested. Although it was an horrific act, it may not have registered on the radar of record keepers or historians of the day due to Bethlehem being a scattered rural community with a small population. It is possible, therefore, that a relatively small number of children were involved, and so the incident may not have come to the attention of the wider world. This atrocity was in keeping with the paranoia which possessed Herod and with his murderous character.

This story reveals three very different reactions to the news that a new King of the Jews had been born. Herod reacted with paranoia, fear and violence. The priests and teachers of the law reacted with indifference. These were the scholars, men who knew the prophecies. They should have been excited, intrigued, joyful when the Magi came asking questions about a newly born King, but instead they were apathetic. Not one of them went to Bethlehem to explore for themselves the possibility of the Messiah being born in fulfilment of the ancient scriptures. Finally, there were the Magi. These were men from another nation, a different culture, who travelled for miles to seek Him, and who, when they found Him, knelt at His cradle and presented Him with Kingly gifts.

How will the world respond this Christmas time to the wonderful news of the birth of Christ? Sadly there are many who will be unbelieving, indifferent or disinterested. May the Holy Spirit of God fall afresh upon the world that the eyes of the blind will be open to see His light of salvation.

The coming of the Christ child was declared to the world by a declaration of nature through the brilliance of a star. The Magi were the first of many drawn to Him from nobility and royalty, throughout every generation in the history of the world, to kneel before Him, fulfilling the beautiful prophecy "Arise, shine for Your light has come. The glory of the Lord appears over You. Nations will come to Your light, and Kings to the brightness of Your dawn." (k)

Let us come to the cradle of Christ this Christmas with the faith of the Magi, declaring: "Unto us a child is born, to us a son is given, and the government will be on his shoulders. He will be called Wonderful Counsellor, Mighty God,

Everlasting Father, Prince of Peace". (j)

This is our God

Scripture References

a)   Matthew 2: 1 – 2

b)   http://www.notablebiographies.com

c)   Matthew 2: 5 – 6

d)   Luke 2: 7 – 8

e)   Hebrews 4: 14

f)   Romans 8: 34

g)   Matthew 2: 12

h)   Hosea 11: 1

i)   Matthew 2: 16 – 18

j)   Isaiah 9: 6

k)   Isaiah 60: 3

10 *Eternity breaks into Time and Space*

The first Christmas morning saw eternity burst into time and space. The perfect union of divinity and humanity, a meeting of the heavenly and earthly realms. Christ came into this world not as a messenger of God, not as a representative of God, but as the perfect reflection of who God is. Jesus makes what is invisible visible. To gaze upon the Son is to gaze upon the Father.

God came to us as a new born child, a baby that changed the universe, a love that was so very gentle, not forced upon us, but offered to us, ever present, waiting to be received, a love that is within the grasp of every man woman and child.

Just as Christ entered into this world, He desires to enter into us, to dwell within us so that we may see with His eyes, think His thoughts, embrace the world with His love.

He clothed Himself in flesh, that we may be clothed in divinity. He made Himself poor that we may share in the riches of His glory. He limited Himself to an earthly life that we may share in the hidden wonders and abundance of eternity. This is our God, the Christ child, the light of the world.

Whatever we are going through, or whatever we face in the future, the light of Christ is constant. It is not possible for darkness to overcome light. Christ will never leave us, He will never fail us, He will always love us. This is why we shall never be bereft of hope. He is the good news. He is joy to the world.

In His earthly life Christ changed lives, and He brought healing. He brought wholeness, and, from brokenness, He brought beauty. Whatever He was He still is, and He evermore shall be.

"Turn your eyes upon Jesus, look full on His wonderful face. And the things of earth will grow strangely dim, in the light of His glory and grace. "

May the beauty and truth of Christ fill your hearts and your homes this Christmas and may you always know that you and yours are kept in His abundant love.

"For God so loved the world that He gave His one and only Son, that whoever believes in Him, shall not perish, but have eternal life". (a)

Thanks be to God

Scripture References
1) John 3: 16

At The Advent of a New Year

When we stand on the threshold of a New Year, it is with both hopes and fears, and this brings to mind the words of the carol: "Oh little town of Bethlehem….. the hopes and fears of all the years are met in Thee tonight."

Hope and fear seem to go together hand in glove. We fear for loved ones who may have been reckless in the past, and we hope that they will make better choices in the future. We are gripped by fear for those who are ill, and vulnerable. We pray for healing to come, for new strength to be given that they may be strong and well and able to embrace life. We fear the breakdown of our precious family life, and we hope and pray for reconciliation, for mutual trust that leads to new beginnings.

The place to bring all of our hopes and our fears is to our God, who is not only our Father, but who is also like a Mother. This is God's word to us in the book of Isaiah: "As a Mother comforts her child, so I will comfort you". (a) Can we find a greater friend than one who reaches out to us in our greatest need, longing to comfort us. This is our God.

We go into the new year with a pioneer going
before us; this is our Christ.   A pioneer goes
where no-one else has gone before, paving the way
for others to come after Him.   A Pioneer is willing
to endure extreme suffering making it easier for His
followers. All of Christ's suffering was for us, and
it was not the end of His story; it was the beginning
of something new and wonderful. His suffering was
the gateway to eternity.

The suffering of Christ assures us that even though
we too must suffer, it is not God's final word. The
final word is hope, a hope that is sure and certain,
made possible through the resurrection of Jesus and
the new life that He promises us.   This new year,
like every year, will bring its joys and its sorrows.
None of us knows what lies ahead. However, when
we reflect on the journey of our past, at every twist
and turn, God was with us.

 The following words are from "Footprints in the
Sand", by Mary Stevenson.

"I walked with God in the sand, and saw two sets of footprints, but I noticed that at times of great difficulty there was only one. I asked God why, in the greatest trials of my life, did He leave me. God replied: "My precious child, I love you and I will never leave you. During times of trial and suffering, when you see only one set of footprints, it was then that I carried you".

We go into this new year with confidence in who God is. He is wisdom, truth, goodness and love. We go forward in hope, our confidence firmly rooted in the God whose love has cradled us all the days of our lives and who promises to be with us to the end.

I said to the man who stood at the Gate of the Year,

"Give me a light that I may tread safely into the unknown."

And he replied, "Go out into the darkness, and put your hand into the hand of God.

That shall be to you better than light, and safer than a known way." (b)

May that Almighty Hand guide and uphold us all.

Scripture References
a)   Isaiah 66: 13
b)   "At the gate of the year" by Minnie Louise Haskins

ABOUT THE AUTHOR

Janice Andrews is the Minister of Musselburgh Congregational Church near Edinburgh in Scotland. She was brought up in Cumnock, where her mother, an inspirational lady, still lives. She shares her home with Pippa, her beloved dog, and is devoted to her young grandchildren, Lewis and Lauren.

Janice recently recorded a series of sermons, which were broadcast by BBC Radio Scotland, on their popular Sunday morning show "New Every Sunday".

She is delighted to receive comments and feedback on any comments or questions about this book, and can be contacted through the church website:

www.musselburghcongregational.org.uk

Made in the USA
Columbia, SC
22 November 2017

It's All About Jesus

When Time Met Infinity

Janice Andrews

DEDICATION

These reflections are dedicated to the memory of my dearest and life long friend, Rev. Matthew Sullivan, former much loved Minister of Cumnock Congregational Church for many years. Rev. Sullivan was a man of faith, a man of prayer, a man of the people, and truly a man of God.